visions of para

the japanese garden in the uk

an exhibition by the japanese garden society

Panorama of Suizen-ji, Kumamoto City, Kyushu. Such gardens in Japan have influenced the design and development of Japanese-style gardens in the UK (IC).

contents

introduction

This catalogue contains text and images from the Japanese Garden Society's exhibition 'Visions of Paradise – the Japanese Garden in the UK', first displayed in 2010 in collaboration with the Embassy of Japan in London.

Inspiration for creating Japanese-style gardens in the UK has naturally come from the gardens of Japan. In order to provide the context for gardens in the UK, the first section of the exhibition is concerned with the gardens of Japan, covering styles, aspects of design, history and illustrating some important gardens. The aim is to set the scene, to provide the background for how we interpret such gardens in a UK setting.

Gardens in the UK and Ireland are covered in three sections: firstly the development of gardens following the opening of Japan to the world in the 1850s, through to the gardens of today; secondly issues relating to cultural borrowing, of using ideas from another culture; and finally a selection of gardens open to the public in the UK and Ireland today.

LEFT: Lanterns outside a stone-mason's yard near the Noguchi Museum in Takamatsu on the island of Shikoku (GH).

the gardens of japan

- garden styles
- twelve important gardens in japan
- aspects of the japanese garden
- a timeline of japanese gardens

the gardens of japan

There is no set formula which constitutes a Japanese garden. When one visits Japan it becomes immediately obvious that the range of gardens is vast, from tiny landscaped spaces outside contemporary apartment blocks to historic Imperial gardens which spread over many acres. Despite this huge range they are all linked by the continuity of a long tradition going back over 1400 years.

Gardens exist in similar places to our own country – attached to houses, both small and large, and as courtyard gardens in hotels, offices, and public buildings. Yet many gardens also exist within the precincts of temples or shrines, something we do not find in the UK. Many of these gardens are of historic value.

Gardens in Japan are of two distinct types: those that are experienced by walking round them and those that are simply viewed from a building or verandah.

Gardeners in Japan are trained today in the same manner as has been practiced for centuries. Apprentices generally study for ten years or more under recognised Master Gardeners, learning and absorbing both technique and respect for history through practical experience. This in part contributes to the remarkable sense of continuity which is discernible throughout the garden tradition.

garden styles

At its heart the Japanese garden remains an attempt by humans to encapsulate the spirit of Nature, recognising the cycle of seasonal changes and the transience of life. The original conception of the garden was to create an idyllic environment that would tempt the deities down from heaven to dwell in proximity to human beings. There are myriad ways in which this over-riding aim has been expressed.

It is perhaps a Western trait to seek categorisation in art of all kinds, although attempts to categorise gardens are inherently restrictive and frequently impossible. However, certain design styles can be identified, whether the garden is an expression of one or several of them.

These general styles have distinct characteristics, defined not only by appearance but also by the size and purpose of the garden.
They are:

- Pond and island gardens
- Dry landscape gardens (karesansui)
- Stroll gardens (kaiyushiki teien)
- Tea Gardens (cha niwa)
- Courtyard gardens (tsubo niwa)

Although 'gardens' appears in these titles, it is often the case that only part of a garden may be in that style. Stroll gardens in particular may contain several of the other styles.

The pond at Ryoan-ji temple, Kyoto, constructed in the 11th century, contains an island (the bridge to it is seen left of centre) which now houses a small Shinto shrine. The ancient pine tree leaning out over the pond is supported on massive props (GH).

pond and island gardens

These are the oldest types of garden to be found in Japan. These are gardens that were meant to be seen both from the interior of buildings as well as whilst walking around them. Such gardens can cover several acres and the pond was often made large enough to accommodate boating excursions (a popular activity particularly in the 10th and 11th centuries)

The islands in the pond were considered sacred spaces, representations of heaven, often with bridges to them from the sides of the pond. In evoking the sense of a complete landscape, the garden around the pond would often feature areas of raised ground depicting mountains or hills.

The gardens were often laid out in accordance with geomantic considerations, for example, the orientation of water inlets and outlets, as well as the position of features such as important stone arrangements.

This garden style also featured in Jodo ('Pureland') temple gardens (11th and 12th centuries) where the garden was a deliberate attempt to create a paradisial world separated from the cares and concerns of the human world.

dry landscape gardens (karesansui)

These gardens are particularly associated with Zen temples and are so-called because sand or gravel is used to represent water. (Karesansui means literally 'dry mountain water'.) This approach was adopted in the 13th century in locations where there was no ready supply of water for a real pond.

Such gardens vary from extreme simplicity to well furnished spaces. Gravel, raked in a variety of ways, is a common ground cover treatment, representing the ocean.

Generally these gardens are not entered but are viewed from a building or verandah. In this way the garden becomes framed by architectural elements.

The moods of the gardens vary from the visually dramatic to the contemplative. An overall connection with Chinese landscape paintings is unmistakable. This garden style has become emblematic of a sense of modernity, despite many such gardens being hundreds of years old.

A karesansui garden at Ryotan-ji temple, Hikone, Shiga Prefecture (GH).

stroll gardens (kaiyushiki teien)

These are gardens which are intended to be viewed as the visitor walks or strolls around them. They retain a link to the original 'pond and island' model of garden, frequently being centred round a large pond, often with a convoluted shoreline.
This style is a carefully created overlapping series of views or vistas, revealed as the viewer progresses around the garden. These views may contain features such as buildings, often based on tea house architecture, the same building being seen in several views from different viewpoints. Some will be bounded by heavy planting or even landforms to create a sense of enclosure. Others will use shakkei, or 'borrowed landscape' as part of the view.
In many gardens it was fashionable to recreate well-known beauty spots, both from within Japan and from China. These would be known to the educated classes from sources such as poetry. The symbolic representation of far distant landscape scenery allowed visitors to travel in their imagination whilst touring the garden.

TOP: The magnificent Imperial garden at Katsura Rikyu in Kyoto is viewed by visitors as they stroll around it, revealing many different views (GH).

RIGHT: Visitors to Jikko-in Temple, Ohara, near Kyoto, may step down from the verandah into the garden to stroll around it, wearing the garden slippers provided (GH).

tea gardens (cha niwa)

Tea gardens came into their own in the 16th century under the guidance of tea masters such as Sen no Rikyu. Essentially the tea garden is a path or roji (literally 'dewy path'), which leads the visitor from the outer 'everyday' world to the tea house and is often composed with stepping stones. The path winds through naturalistic planting, often with a ground covering of verdant moss, the aesthetic intention being to recreate the mood of a simple path through a mountain glade. Colour is eschewed in preference to shades of green.

The garden may be divided into two parts - the outer and inner gardens - adding to a sense of progression. Guests will wait in the outer garden in a waiting arbour or machiai, and when called by the host to the tea house will walk through the garden, pausing at a water basin illuminated by a stone lantern. Here they will scoop a little water over their hands symbolising the cleansing of body and mind before entering the tea house in a state of readiness for the social interchange of the tea ceremony.

TOP: Stepping-stone path through a tea garden, Koto-in temple, Kyoto (GH).

LEFT: Water basin typical of a tea garden, Daichi-ji, Shiga Prefecture (GH).

ABOVE: A tiny tsubo-niwa between buildings at Fukuchi-in, Koya-san, a modern design by Shigemori Mirei (GH)

Tsubo niwa are gardens in relatively small spaces found between buildings. They can be among the residences of the aristocracy, in temples, as well as in the more secular settings of traditional merchants' houses in cities such as Kyoto. If there is a continuity of character in these gardens it is that they appear as 'fragments' of gardens, which nevertheless are capable of standing alone. Town house architecture developed a pattern of dwellings long and narrow in their footprint. In order to allow light and fresh air to circulate, the architecture was punctuated with small spaces which could be developed as garden areas (tsubo niwa). These were generally viewed from surrounding rooms or above from the first floor. The gardens were visually centred on a stone water basin, or well; planting being minimal in the shaded conditions.
Some larger town houses and modern suburban houses have front garden spaces. Lanterns, rocks and planting are laid out in an informal manner. A tall wall, hedge or fence separates the property from the street and provides a sense of enclosure.

BELOW: A garden within a merchant's house in Nara. This space lies between two halves of the property, with a connecting covered walkway to one side. The other side is the wall of the next door house, thus containing the garden space within the property, unseen by outsiders (GH).

twelve important gardens in japan

Selecting gardens to highlight is inevitably a subjective process at some level. Everyone who visits Japan will have their favourite gardens. The gardens selected here are among dozens that could be described as 'important'. These twelve gardens are in no particular order, but have been chosen because they show both geographic spread and range of history and style.

1. Mōtsū-ji (Osawa, Hiraizumi, Iwate)

Built in the Heian period about 1000 years ago this is probably the best surviving example of a garden from that time (IC).

2. Kenroku-en (Kanazawa, Ishikawa)

A stroll garden originally built in 1676 for a clan chieftain, it is one of the three 'Great gardens of Japan'. The image shows pine tree branches being held by ropes against the weight of heavy snow, a means of protection put in place every November on hundreds of trees around Kanazawa (GH).

3. Katsura Rikyu (Kyoto)

A magnificent stroll garden constructed during the 17th century. Now managed by the Imperial Household Agency it represents the pinnacle of design for this style of garden (GH).

4. Ryōan-ji (Kyoto)

Perhaps the most famous of the karesansui gardens, the mysterious arrangement of 15 stones in a field of raked gravel has captured the imaginations of generations of visitors. Now a World Heritage site, it is thought to have been built in the early 16th century - although this date is disputed by some scholars (GH).

5. Tōfuku-ji (Kyoto)

In 1939 Shigemori Mirei built four gardens around the Hojo (Main Hall) of the Tofuku-ji temple in Kyoto. The style was seen as very radical at the time and caused great controversy. This small garden on the north side of the building has become something of an iconic image in recent times (GH).

6. Murin-an (Kyoto)

Completed in 1895 by Ogawa Jihei, this garden was a breakthrough in style, being very naturalistic in ways that echo gardens in the west. The borrowed scenery (Shakkei) of the eastern hills is very effective (IC).

7. Kishiwada-jo (Kishiwada, Osaka)

The stone arrangement, designed by Shigemori Mirei in 1953, suggests both the castle's old fortification walls and a battle scene from Chinese mythology. Shigemori was a great innovator, here introducing linear geometric shapes (GH).

8. Ritsurin-koen (Takamatsu, Kagawa)

This huge stroll garden is typical of gardens created for the daimyo or clan chieftains in the first hundred years of the Edo period, reflecting the peaceful nature of the times (GH).

9. Kōraku-en (Okayama)

Completed in 1700 this is one of three 'Great gardens of Japan'. A huge stroll garden below Okayama castle, it incorporates extensive use of lawned areas, and has changed relatively little since it was built (GH).

10. The Adachi Museum (Yasugi, Shimane)

The immaculately maintained gardens of the Adachi Museum, completed during the 1980s, are considerably smaller than they look, so good is the illusion created. The expansive view of the mountains makes it seem as if they are a continuation of the garden (GH).

11. Shukkei-en (Hiroshima)

Created in 1620 for a clan chieftain, Shukkei-en now offers a haven of tranquility in the heart of the city. After suffering considerable damage the gardens were re-opened in 1951 (GH).

12. Suizen-ji (Kumamoto, Kyushu)

This garden was built in 1636 as a tea retreat, but is now located in a public park. The image of Mount Fuji is unmistakable, and was a popular feature in gardens of the period (IC).

aspects of the japanese garden

Defining what constitutes a Japanese garden is difficult, yet we all know one when we see it. One way of approaching a definition is to consider various aspects of the gardens in Japan that differ from those in the West. This enables us to understand better how we can borrow ideas from this different culture in a more successful way in our own country.

There are many potential aspects to consider. These include how the viewer engages with the garden, how the garden is designed as a whole rather than a series of separate entities, how views are presented to the viewer and how design takes inspiration from landscape painting. Attention to detail in design and maintenance is another aspect of difference, as is the use of apparently empty space within the gardens. Some gardens 'borrow' external scenery as an extension of the garden space. In most gardens there is a limited palette of colours used and symbolism often plays a part in the design. Above all, it is the manner in which natural materials, particularly rocks and water, are used that distinguishes them from their European counterparts.

OPPOSITE: Detail of the garden at Raikyu-ji, Takahashi, Okayama Prefecture (GH)

composition and wholeness

One of the most important aspects of design in the Japanese garden tradition is the manner in which the garden space comes together as a single entity. The garden space is seen as a whole, being made up of the interrelation of various elements, as opposed to the garden being a series of elements simply gathered together to create the whole. It is a subtle but important distinction; each element of the garden has a purpose, justified within the overall concept. No element of design will be secondary; rockwork flows together forming the 'skeleton' of the garden, and the planting is set out as the 'flesh on the bones', each element determined by the other. In order to achieve this, the designer will often perceive the garden with the eyes of an artist, painter or sculptor. In Zen temple gardens, for example, there is a heightened form of interdependence of elements in the garden. The garden components are pared down to leave only those elements that are absolutely necessary; nothing extraneous is allowed.

TOP: Each element in this scene at the Imperial Palace garden in central Kyoto contributes to the overall scene (GH).

RIGHT: Many elements, textures and forms make up this scene in the garden of Jikko-in temple in Ohara near Kyoto, including the borrowed scenery of the mountain (GH).

RIGHT: The entrance path to Koto-in temple in Kyoto leads the visitor to wonder what will come, what is round the corner. Nothing is revealed until then, thereby engaging the viewer and allowing them to feel they are leaving the everyday world behind (IC).

BELOW: This intimate scene at Jikko-in temple, Ohara, near Kyoto, engages the viewer from the verandah. The use of space draws the viewer into the scene, which changes as they move along the verandah (GH).

engagement - the viewer and the viewed

A Japanese garden is a carefully managed visual environment, always at the centre of which is the viewer. The central concern when creating a garden in Japan is the question of how the viewer will interact with it.

For a garden to function well, the viewer needs to be drawn into the garden and become part of the experience as a whole. Most contemporary Western gardens have lost sight of this ideal, being concerned more with display rather than engagement.

In gardens that are entered, the viewer is often presented an unfolding series of views as they progress around the garden. In this way the viewer engages with the garden through the various views presented, each of which builds into the whole experience of the garden.

In gardens that are not entered, being viewed from either a raised verandah or from within an interior, the imagination of the viewer is captured by the scene presented. By moving along the verandah different views unfold, where the architecture frames the scene.

In the Japanese garden the viewer is drawn into the fabric of the garden, thereby creating a deep sense of intimacy and involvement. The viewer and the garden are drawn into a harmonious whole.

gardens and landscape painting

Japanese garden design was strongly influenced by the aesthetics and techniques of Chinese landscape painting, avidly collected and studied in Japan. The painter's depiction of landscape was not so much to mimic nature, rather to show the essence of landscape. Thus the scenery presented to the viewer was a highly refined vision of nature.

The Japanese garden, being also a study in the expression of a vision of Nature, similarly seeks to reflect the essence of Nature in a refined and concentrated manner. Garden creators are unhindered by the painter's limitation of working in two dimensions; they are also able to work with the dimension of depth, and, beyond that, the dimension of time through the effects of seasonal change and development. This makes a garden composition potentially a highly charged and complex work of art, and one that is capable of great subtlety.

TOP: The Yellow Mountains (Huang Shan) in China have been a source of inspiration for generations of landscape painters (RK).

RIGHT: The garden at Daisen-in temple in Kyoto shows very strong links to Chinese landscape painting (GH).

composing with views

The Japanese garden can be considered to be a series of interrelated views, at the hub of which is the viewer or visitor to the garden. A view can be understood to be composed of three distinct parts: foreground, middleground and background. Each part will lead on toward the next, thus creating a view or scene as a visually logical whole. What become important are the 'empty' spaces which bind these three elements together.

In the stroll garden much use is made of a technique referred to as 'hide and reveal' (meigakure), where subtly controlled views are opened and closed as the viewer progresses around the garden. The garden is therefore experienced sequentially, as if stepping through one visual scenario into another; a technique adapted from Chinese landscape paintings.

TOP: A view framed by a picture window at the Adachi Museum of Art, Yasugi, Shimane Prefecture (GH).

LEFT: This alignment of stones leading to the Buddhist triad includes the viewer in the scene. Komyo-in temple, Kyoto (GH).

RIGHT: A view of the garden at Chishaku-in, Kyoto allowing the architecture to frame the scene (GH).

yohaku, the mystery of empty space

In Chinese and Japanese art, empty space is perceived as a positive force, rather than being simply a void. Emptiness or white space (yohaku) is considered to reveal the opposite; form. For example, it is the spaces between the pads of foliage of a pine which gives definition to the tree.

The use of yohaku as a positive design element is derived from Chinese landscape painting, and its manipulation is one of the most complex and compelling aspects of Japanese gardens. A contemporary Japanese master gardener likened the creation of a garden "to excavating holes in a solid block of matter, revealing more and more yohaku, until the true nature of things becomes apparent."

Each element separated by yohaku brings order and identity to the other. Form, of itself, is inherently limited, therefore by using 'emptiness' as a balancing agent the potential of creating a garden space without apparent limits is unleashed.

TOP: Space between foreground, middle-ground and background works to make this Imperial garden at Shugaku-in, Kyoto, seem much larger than it really is (GH).

RIGHT: Empty space between the branches, created by careful pruning, reveals the form of the tree. Koko-en gardens, Himeji, Hyōgo Prefecture (GH).

OPPOSITE: A pine branch pruned to reach out over a pond at Shuraku-en, Tsuyama, Okayama Prefecture. Consistent pruning underneath has revealed the branch structure. (GH)

a question of colour

There has long been a preference in Chinese and Japanese art towards the monochrome. Black is not viewed as being a negation of colour; rather it holds the potential of all colours to exist in the imagination. The Japanese garden with an overwhelming preponderance of evergreen plant material presents, at first viewing, a uniform and bland palette. The richness lies in the detail of the forms and the subtle shading of tones of colour.

In the Japanese garden bright colours are used in a concentrated, directed manner, in particular to highlight seasonal shifts. Thus in spring the garden may dazzle when cherry blossom, azalea or iris flower, and again in the autumn with the turning of maple leaves. During the period of summer heat and humidity, the garden reveals myriad shades of deep calm cooling greens. Colour is indicative of the seasons and seasonal change and limiting its use enhances its visual impact, whilst retaining purpose to its use.

TOP: Flowering Azaleas at the Old Furukawa Garden in Tokyo. Clipped Azaleas do flower and in some gardens are left to flower freely before being clipped again as the flowers fade, leaving the plant time to develop buds for the following year (GH).

LEFT: Autumn colour on *Acer palmatum* trees at the Moss Temple, Saiho-ji, Kyoto (GH)

OPPOSITE: Cherry blossom (Sakura) against a background of pruned Cryptomeria at Ryoan-ji, Kyoto. (GH)

use of symbolism in the garden

In Japanese gardens it is not uncommon to find symbolism and reference woven into the composition. As representations of an imagined paradise, and being inspired by poetry and poetic thought, references are made to many mythical ideas. Among these are turtle and crane islands (both important symbols associated with longevity), the Isles of the Immortals, as well as sundry sacred mountains being evoked in the imaginary landscapes of the garden. The creative benefit of weaving symbolism into a garden composition comes through the greater potential for engaging the viewer.

The Japanese garden is very rich in meaning, be it grand themes or allusions of a more personal, local resonance; the garden actively seeks to communicate with the viewer. It comes as no surprise to find gardens in Buddhist temples incorporating a rich variety of symbolic content from the Buddhist cosmology.

TOP: A garden stone symbolising a boat at Ryotan-ji temple, Hikone, Shiga Prefecture (GH).

LEFT: A gourd shaped water basin at Reiun-in temple, Tofuku-ji, Kyoto. The gourd symbolises good luck, longevity and fecundity (GH).

attention to detail

Attention to detail is of paramount importance in both the creation and maintenance of Japanese gardens. Judging what is 'right', what 'works', is assessed through feeling and intuition based on long experience. Garden creators pay great attention to detail in seeking an apparent complete 'naturalness', by hiding the hand of the designer in creating scenery that is rooted in a naturalistic expressionism.

Much attention is given to the detail of the manner in which the garden will be viewed, whether seen from within a building (using the architecture as a framework), or, in the case of larger gardens, where the space is revealed as a sequence of views or vistas.

Great attention to detail applies also to garden maintenance. Being concerned with maintaining the relative balance between garden elements, pruning of shrubs and trees forms an important part of a gardener's work, as does keeping the garden clean and tidy. A well presented and cared for garden makes a deep impression on the viewer.

TOP: Every stone in this man-made cascade has been placed with attention to detail to ensure a natural appearance. Agon-Shu temple, Kyoto (GF).

LEFT: Detail of a bamboo fence made with up to 20 layers of bamboo shoots in a regular pattern. Umeko-ji koen, Kyoto (GH)

water and rocks, yin and yang

Perhaps the most significant aspect that absolutely distinguishes the Japanese garden from its western counterpart is the manner and use of rocks and water in garden composition. These two elements are defining features, indeed the term for 'landscape' in both Chinese and Japanese is created by combining the ideograms for san (山), 'mountain' with sui (水), 'water'.

Water, the essence of life, is found as a motif across the entire spectrum of cultural and artistic expression in Japan. In the East Asian conception, the universe is composed of two opposite, but complementary forces (yin and yang) and it is through the interaction of these fundamental forces that energy and movement (thus life itself) are created. In the context of landscape, yin is most readily recognised in the presence of water, either still or flowing.

Rocks or stones in the garden are elements at the polar opposite to water and are thus seen as an expression of yang. Their very presence indicates weight and mass, something that does not apparently alter its shape or form easily. Yet their very appearance is indicative of the extraordinary forces (temporal and energetic) that conspired in their making.

Rocks used in the garden are symbolic of mountains, and mountains are a link between earth and heaven. Thus they have for millennia been seen and appreciated as indicators of spiritual aspiration and artistic expression beyond time and place.

A strong arrangement of rocks around the pond at Nijo Castle, Kyoto (GH).

shakkei, or borrowed scenery

Shakkei is the technique of incorporating elements from outside the garden as an integral element of the garden composition. Its use relies on there being an element beyond the garden that may be used, be it a view of mountains, a fine building, or even something as simple as a beautiful tree or other such feature. Shakkei is a way of using an external view or feature to give the illusion that the garden extends well beyond its real boundaries.

Various techniques are used to borrow or 'capture' the external scene, often a distinct horizontal line of hedging or a carefully shaped series of shrubs. These act to break the continuum of view whilst acting as a link between the garden and external scenery.

The garden itself is representative of an abstracted landscape and through shakkei a link with the greater landscape is forged. It can reinforce and extend the imaginative journey with which the viewer engages.

TOP: The roof of a nearby temple gateway and the hillside behind are 'borrowed' as an extension of the garden scene. Trees and shrubs exclude the intervening car park from the view. Isui-en, Nara (GH).

LEFT: A carefully screened view of the mountain extends the view at Raikyu-ji temple, Takahashi, Okayama Prefecture (GH).

a time line of japanese gardens

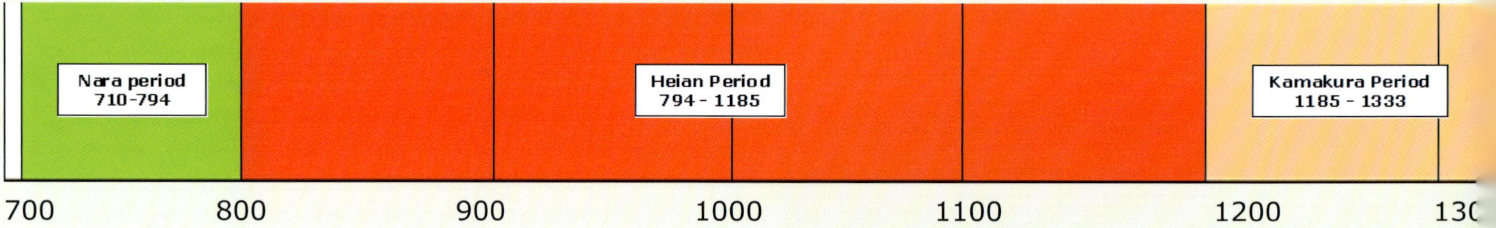

Gardens have been built in Japan since at least the 8th Century and possibly earlier. Based on inspiration from China, the Japanese tradition of garden building developed gradually through the many periods of Japanese history.

This timeline illustrates examples from each of the major periods. Dates for starts and ends o these periods vary slightly in different historical texts. The dates exhibited have been taken from 'Japanese Garden Design' by Marc Peter Keane.

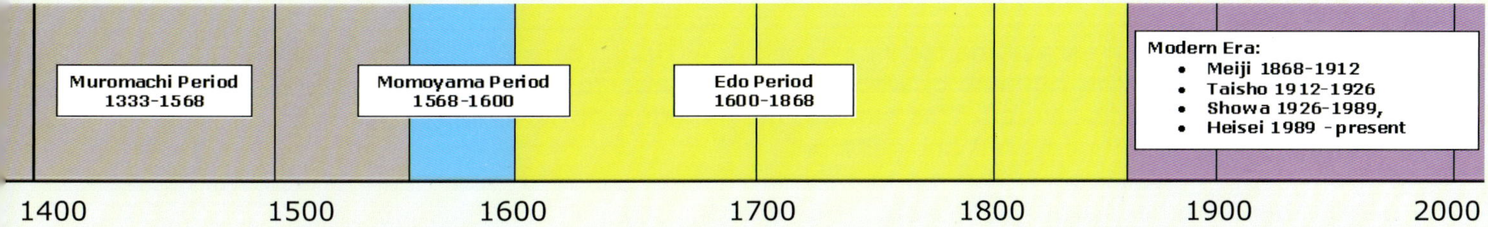

It is worth noting that interest in Japanese gardens in the UK only started during the Meiji Period following the restoration of the Emperor as Head of State in 1868.

The garden at Tatton Park, arguably our most important historical garden, was constructed in 1911. This puts it in the very last section of the timeline, illustrating, very visibly, the long history of gardens in Japan.

Panorama of the Heian Period garden of Motsu-ji, Hiraizumi, Iwate (IC)

Nara Period: 710 - 794

Kyuseki Teien

In the early 1980s, when excavating for a new post-office building in Nara, the remains of what looked like an old garden were discovered. This garden, the Kyuseki teien, was then uncovered and restored. It dates from the mid 8th century. The winding stream course is thought to be typical of the time. The post office was constructed elsewhere (GH).

Heian Period: 794 – 1185

Byodo-in, Uji, Kyoto

A 1000 year old pure-land temple and garden. The architecture and garden were based on Chinese models of the time (GH).

Kamakura Period: 1185 – 1333

Saiho-ji, Kyoto

The site of the Moss Temple (Koke-dera) at Saiho-ji in western Kyoto originally contained many buildings around a pond in the shape of the kanji-character for 'heart'. Within the grounds are two very early stone arrangements from the early 13th century, probably built by Chinese stone arrangers. The area round the lake became coated in moss under the trees, the moss now giving its name to the temple (RK).

Muromachi Period: 1333 – 1568

Tenryu-ji in Kyoto

The garden at Tenryu-ji is thought to be one of the first to use the technique of shakkei in borrowing the view of the Arashiyama hills. Dating from around 1379, the dry waterfall rock arrangement is particularly fine (GH).

Kinkaku-ji, Kyoto

Also known as the 'Golden Temple', Kinkaku-ji, was constructed by Shogun Ashikaga Yoshimitsu in 1397. The original building was burnt down in 1950 in an arson attack, the replica building being coated in gold leaf. The garden, a complex lake with many islands, was typical of its time when boating parties around the lake were highly fashionable (GH).

Muromachi Period: 1333 - 1568

Ginkaku-ji, Kyoto

The pond adjacent to the 'Silver Temple', Ginkaku-ji, was constructed in the 1480s by the Shogun Ashikaga Yoshimasa. The pond and paths around it are on a much more intimate and refined scale than previous gardens, heralding a new direction in garden making (GH).

Katsura Rikyu, Kyoto

The Imperial garden at Katsura Rikyu was constructed in the refined style of the early Edo period. As a stroll garden it is thought to represent the pinnacle of the style (GH).

Edo Period: 1600 - 1868

Raikyu-ji in Takahashi, Okayama

The garden at Raikyu-ji was laid out by the famous garden creator Kobori Enshu in the early 1600s. It is a fine example of gardens of the time, showing a refined approach following the exuberance of the Momoyama period (GH).

Meiji Period: 1868 - 1912

Murin-an, Kyoto

The villa of Murin-an has a garden created in what became a fashionable naturalistic style by Ogawa Jihei. It is thought that the owner of the villa, Yamagata Aritomo, a veteran statesman, had a particular desire to create a new style of garden. Built in the 1890s, Murin-an is seen as the beginning of this new naturalistic style, perhaps incorporating some aesthetic ideas from the West. It made Ogawa Jihei famous and he went on to build many gardens for wealthy villa owners in that part of Kyoto (IC).

Showa Period: 1926 - 1989

Tofuku-ji, Kyoto

The famous chequerboard pattern of stone and moss was created in Tofuku-ji by Shigemori Mirei in what was effectively his first commission to design and build a garden, in 1939. There are four gardens around the Hojo, this one becoming something of an icon in representing the modern Japanese garden (GH).

Matsuo Taisha, Kyoto

Matsuo Taisha has three gardens designed by Shigemori Mirei in the early 1970s (there is a fourth garden built by his son after his death). This one is a modern interpretation of the winding stream popular in the Nara and early Heian periods (See Kyuseki teien, page 34) (GH).

Umeko-ji koen, Kyoto

In 1995, to celebrate the 1200th anniversary of the founding of Kyoto, a new park was built on the site of some disused railway sidings near Kyoto station. In a corner of the park is this modern garden which incorporates western style planting, a current trend in experimental gardens (GH).

garden developments in the uk

- early japanese-style gardens 1850 -1930
- decline and resurgence

Fanhams Hall, Ware, Hertfordshire (GB)

early japanese-style gardens 1850 -1930

introduction

In the West we have known about Chinese gardens for several centuries, but this is not the case with Japan. Until 1868 Japan was a country which had self-imposed political and cultural isolation from the outside world for nearly 250 years. With the opening of Japan's doors to the West, many aspects of Japan's culture created great interest, including their gardens. Within 30 years several 'Japanese' gardens were built here, reaching a peak of interest and activity early in the 20th century.

The early enchantment with Japan saw many visitors travelling there. Plant hunters found that Japan was a rich source of new exotic plants. In the late 19th and early 20th centuries Japan was keen to show the world its culture and did so in a series of world fairs, most importantly for us in the Japan-British Exhibition of 1910.

The early gardens had many different interpretations of what a 'Japanese' garden here meant; evaluation of these through the eyes of the 21st century being different from how they were seen at the time. Many gardens have now disappeared or have left little trace of their original splendour.

enchantment with japan

A hundred years ago the Japanese arts were the height of fashion. Visitors with the necessary wealth flocked to Japan and returned with a compulsion to recreate the gardens they had seen back on their home soil. Shopping mania seemed to grip many, causing them to purchase plants, lanterns, rocks and even live deer to be transported home to Britain. Japanese lanterns remain in gardens to this day as testaments to those overseas adventures but they were not solely the result of foreign travel. In Japan, companies ran a thriving export trade with the gardeners of Britain, seducing overseas buyers with stunningly beautiful catalogues, while in Britain firms such as Gauntlett's specialised in Japanese plants and ornaments.

In 1877, Josiah Conder, a young English architect, went to Japan to teach architecture at the Imperial University. In 1891 he published 'The Flowers of Japan, and the Art of Floral Arrangement', then in 1893 'Landscape Gardening in Japan'. Conder's books were among the first serious studies of the subject to be published in the West, and they became influential and Conder's illustrated book on gardens is still in print today.

plant collectors

Japan was seen from the mid-nineteenth century until well into the twentieth century as a rich source of new plant species for the British Isles, especially since both countries shared similar maritime climates. There was knowledge of the Japanese flora prior to the opening of Japan to the West from the physicians Englebert Kaemfer, Karl Pieter Thunberg and Philip Hans von Siebold, all employed by the Dutch trading concession on the artificial island of Deshima, adjacent to Nagasaki.

After the gunboat diplomacy of the 1850s early visitors to Japan included the plant collectors of nursery firms and botanical gardens, including Robert Fortune and John Gould Veitch. These collectors wrote accounts of their explorations of Japan that featured in the gardening periodicals of the time. Many of the plant species that were sent back successfully found a home in the British garden, and some took on a special significance due to their connections with Japan.

interpretations

The expression of Japanese-style gardens in Britain was extremely diverse ranging from carefully constructed replicas striving for authenticity to a nod to 'the fair Japan' with the addition of such novelties as a random lantern, bridge or plant, to gardens which were solely a collection of Japanese plants. Diplomats with experience of Japan created the early examples of Japanese-style gardens such as Saumarez Park (c.1890), Guernsey, and Heale House (c.1901), Wiltshire. These were filled with authentic items with which their owners had returned from the East, and yet even with the aid of Japanese design consultants, these gardens were poor representations of those in Japan; the various features seeming disconnected from their new settings.

Gardens where there was a greater degree of involvement from a Japanese designer came closest to gaining the appearance of gardens as they would have been found in Japan. The work of Taki Handa and later J. Suzuki at Cowden Castle (1907), Perthshire; of Seyemon Kusumoto's involvement, from 1923, at Cheynes (Cottered), (1906), Hertfordshire, and finally the designs of J. Suzuki at The Node, Hertfordshire (c.1930), and possibly at Trewince, Cornwall (1935) were examples of much stronger and convincing designs.

Early image of the lake at Cowden (Sir Robert Stewart)

The lake at Cowden today, with virtually nothing left of the Japanese garden (J&MR)

Early image of the garden at Cowden (Sir Robert Stewart)

Cowden – The remains of a lantern (J&MR)

LEFT: Taki Handa, designer and supervisor of landscaping, Cowden (Sir Robert Stewart) CENTRE: Matsuo, the gardener at Cowden (Sir Robert Stewart). RIGHT: Gravestone of Matsuo "For 12 years Trusted Keeper of the Japanese Garden Cowden D October 20 1937" (J&MR)

LEFT: Red Bridge at Cottered (J&MR) CENTRE: Professor Suzuki, associated with many early Japanese gardens (Dr Kitamura, granddaughter of Professor Suzuki). RIGHT: Torii gate at Cottered (J&MR)

Evaluating the early gardens

The early Japanese-style gardens of Britain are only just beginning to receive the attention they deserve. However they are often considered to lack a resemblance to the refined gardens of Japan. This questing for authenticity by the modern viewer has devalued many of these gardens, the presumption having been that these British creations should be replica copies of those in Japan. This has been to miss the point that gardens away from their native geology, climate, society and culture are almost bound to be different. They tell us far more about the state of British society at the time of their creation; of artistic trends and of horticultural fashions. Most of all these Japanese-style gardens were a celebration of our relationship with Japan.

TOP: Fanhams Hall, Hertfordshire, where the Japanese garden was laid out in 1900-1901 by Professor Suzuki (J&MR).

RIGHT: Private Garden, Kent. Constructed in the early 1920s and based on a design from Josiah Conder's Landscape Gardening in Japan. (IC).

gardens of the japan-british exhibition of 1910

The latter part of the nineteenth century saw a series of international exhibitions in Britain, mainland Europe and the United States. It was these exhibitions that were to become the showcase for the Japanese garden in the West. The Japan-British Exhibition of 1910 at White City in London attracted over eight million visitors in just a six-month period, with two major gardens constructed to display the skills of Japanese landscapers.

The 'Garden of Peace' was much admired due to its high standard of finish and the surrounding panorama that prevented intruding views. The 'Garden of the Floating Islands' was considered "well designed and eminently attractive" (The Gardeners' Magazine, 1910, 21 May: 386).

Most of the Exhibition site has now been built on; BBC Television Centre occupying part of what was the Garden of Peace. The remaining section of this garden still exists as Hammersmith Park and recently has been 're-imagined' as a collaboration between the Japanese and British landscape architects.

RIGHT: Six of the many postcards produced for the Exhibition (IC).

JAPAN-BRITISH
EXHIBITION
Garden of Peace.

Garden of Peac
In the Japanese Gardens,
Japan-British Exhibition, London, 1910.
671.

Court of Progress, Japan-British Exhibition
572

Garden of Peace, Japan-British Exhibition

conservation

Where are these gardens now? A few are well known and cared for such as the Japanese-style garden at Tatton Park, Cheshire, but the majority are lost, hidden under encroaching undergrowth and suffering the effects of neglect, vandalism or the sale of the more valuable ornaments.

Historical authenticity seems to raise a particular area of concern for the Japanese-style garden. Sometimes the allure of Japan still seems to hold a magnetic force and gardens are 'restored' to a 'Japanese' model that was not envisaged by a past designer. The Japanese-style gardens of the British Isles need to be viewed, as far as possible, through the eyes of their contemporary creators, builders and garden visitors, both for their accurate restoration and for an understanding of the complex history they represent.

TOP: Tatton Park during construction, 1910/11 (Sam Youd, Tatton Park).

RIGHT and OPPOSITE: Tatton Park following the 2001 restoration (GH).

decline and resurgence

introduction

By the mid 20th century Japanese gardens were wholly out of fashion. Many existing gardens had been left to decay or were destroyed. Only a few have survived, two that are now open to the public are Tatton Park (1910) and Compton Acres (1922).
By the late '60s and early '70s an interest in Japanese gardens began to re-emerge in the UK and Europe. With the developing demand for stylish, low maintenance gardens, more and more garden creators began to incorporate ideas from Japan into Western gardens. Today it is not unusual to see rocks, stone waterbasins, stepping stone paths, gravel areas, cloud-pruned shrubs and so on in their designs.
During the last 50 years many new Japanese-style gardens have been built in the UK, some of which are open to the public. Most of these are smaller and less ambitious than the earlier gardens. Today the interest in and awareness of Japanese gardens is probably stronger than ever. The Japanese Garden Society has several hundred members in the UK alone, and the number of Japanese style gardens in the UK is increasing all the time.

evaluating recent gardens

As in earlier times it is perhaps unfortunate that many gardens have been labelled 'Japanese' that fail to capture the true feeling of a garden in Japan. Undoubtedly those that have been created by someone well versed in the Japanese tradition are more likely to be representative of the real thing. Having said that, if a garden is aesthetically pleasing and viewers find it interesting, absorbing, calming, then it can be said to work, however authentic or otherwise it happens to be.
Meticulous maintenance, as such gardens would receive in Japan, is undoubtedly an issue in the UK. It is often overlooked, to the detriment of the garden and our appreciation of it. Ray Townsend, Arboretum Manager at Kew Gardens, comments that previously they attempted to cope with a low level of maintenance effort, but found that it didn't work. When they did get around to pruning, they were taking so much off that the plants took some weeks or months to recover. They have now adopted weekly sessions, with light trims everywhere it is needed, plus usual tidying and raking. It is absorbing a much higher maintenance effort than any other part of the Arboretum, but the results are very positive.

OPPOSITE: The Japanese garden at Kew Gardens (Royal Botanic Gardens, Kew)

TOP: Hammersmith – turtle arrangement in the play area in the renovated garden at Hammersmith Park (GB).

TOP RIGHT: Hammersmith - remodelled water course in the renovated Garden of Peace from the 1910 Japan-British Exhibition – now in Hammersmith Park (GB).

RIGHT: Private garden in Manchester designed and built by a member of the Japanese Garden Society (GH).

TOP: A dry waterfall in the new Japanese garden at Kew, built in 1996 (GB).

RIGHT: Japanese Garden in Silver End Memorial Garden, Braintree. Built in 1948 (J&MR).

TOP: The Momotaro garden of War at Spalding, Lincolnshire, built in 2004 (TB).

TOP RIGHT: The Momotaro garden of Peace at Spalding, Lincolnshire, built in 2004 (TB).

RIGHT: Willowbrook Hospice, St Helens, Merseyside. The Garden of Reflection and Reconciliation, designed and constructed by volunteers from the JGS in 2009 (GH).

TOP: The Japanese Garden Society garden designed by Maureen Busby at the RHS Chelsea Flower Show in 2004, gaining a Gold Medal (MB).

RIGHT: The Japanese Garden Society Courtyard garden designed by Maureen Busby at the RHS Hampton Court Show 2002, gaining a Gold Medal and 'Best in Show' (MB).

cultural borrowing

The very notion of creating a 'Japanese style garden' raises many interesting questions, not least whether it is possible at all to create a 'Japanese garden' outside of its geographical and cultural origins. Attempting even a partial answer draws us into considering the very notion of what constitutes a garden and what its function is in the wider cultural context. Much of the development of a gardener in Japan, apart from basic horticultural skills, involves a training of the eye. To see plants and rocks as dynamic sculptural forms, to develop a sensitivity to the layout of the garden's components is fundamental. This way of viewing the garden is one of the significant distinguishing features between the two garden cultures.

In interpreting Japanese garden ideas in the UK it is therefore pertinent to look again at the tradition as a whole, to look beyond surface appearances towards the potential being offered. By understanding what lies behind the outward appearance we stand a better chance of drawing the greatest benefit from the study and appreciation of another culture.

Many 'Japanese style' gardens have been created in this country, varying from the loosest connection (a curved red bridge arching over a pond or a stone lantern set in a flower border), to more serious and high-minded attempts to recreate the manner of gardens that may be seen in Japan itself. Interpretation depends greatly on the garden creator's experience and knowledge of the Japanese garden tradition. When looking at older gardens another dependency is the time when they were built and the prevailing fashionable notions of that time. What might have been the height of fashion in a 'Japanese garden' in the 1920s is different from our view today.

Further, what is 'Japanese' is changing all the time. Modern design in Japan has adopted and adapted many aspects of design from the West. As design becomes more international, or trans-national, many elements of Japanese design principles and practices in all the arts are being adopted throughout the world. The differences between traditional design approaches in the two cultures are breaking down.

TOP: Compton Acres - built in the 1920s as a private 'oriental' garden incorporating Chinese-style and Japanese-style buildings and artefacts, displayed regardless of how such objects would be used in their native culture. Nevertheless, this is an attractive garden in a lovely setting (GH).

RIGHT: Cottered – The red bridge at Nikko in Japan was seen as something really 'Japanese' and therefore to be incorporated into many Japanese-style gardens here (GB).

tradition

In Japan, the exercise of creating gardens commenced in the 7th century and has evolved into a highly sophisticated tradition. The Western garden (in the modern sense) is by comparison relatively new. One characteristic of the development of a tradition is that innovation and cumulative change occur relatively slowly. In the West, where garden innovation has been subject more to changing notions of taste and fashion, developments have occurred at a much quicker pace. In the Japanese tradition there is a deliberate richness and ambiguity of meaning. The Western view (especially in the visually dominated post modern world) primarily strives to be transparent and literal in its expression.

TOP: Pruned Japanese White Pine at Jiko-in, near Nara, Japan. This illustrates the attention to detail over generations of gardeners to create such trees. It is difficult for us to recreate such plant material in our culture (GH).

RIGHT: Pruning a pine tree (2 men 2 days), Yushi-en near Matsue, Shimane Prefecture (GH).

In the tradition of garden creation in Japan there is a clear and unhindered expression of the original notion of the garden itself. That is the garden representing sacred space; a place where humans may interact with the forces of Nature, and in so doing be able to connect more profoundly with that which sustains us. Gardens in Japan are an expression of the notion of Paradise, or an idealised state or condition. Manifested as idealised landscapes, they are fundamentally different from the perception of gardens in the UK, despite similarly being rooted in the quest to represent Paradise. Different cultural influences have led to a different interpretation in the form and substance of our gardens.

TOP and RIGHT: Private garden in Hertfordshire (Sylvana) showing an amalgam of Japanese ideas of use of space with mixed planting in European style (GB).

the influence of 'zen'

In the UK, indeed throughout the west, it has become very popular to look to East Asia for creative inspiration. Without proper study this can lead to misunderstandings and misinterpretations. For example, the word 'Zen' has become synonymous to many with Japan and Japanese culture. The word is frequently used as a shorthand term to denote a certain style that has associations with minimalism, brevity, abstraction, et cetera. Often the word is used in a context completely disassociated from its origin as a particular form of Buddhism.
Hence a 'Zen-style garden' often designates one composed primarily of a gravel ground-cover, and may or may not also feature rocks or plants. It is its physical constituents that attempt to define it, rather than the cultural context and tradition from which it has arisen.

RIGHT: Private garden in Shropshire – A modern treatment strongly rooted in the Japanese garden tradition. This is an example of modern designers using Japanese ideas in a UK setting with success (GH).

OPPOSITE: Momotaro garden – Spalding, Lincolnshire. A modern garden that tells the story, popular with children in Japan, of Momotaro, the Peach Tree boy. The garden follows the Japanese tradition of telling a story, in this case almost literally following it as you stroll through the garden, with various scenes depicted (TB).

interpretation and authenticity

There are significant differences between Japan and the UK that must be dealt with in creating a Japanese-style garden here: climate, architecture, landscape, plant material and attitude to maintenance. All of these affect the interpretation of Japanese ideas and make an 'authentic' garden virtually impossible. Perhaps the closest to an authentic appearance is a pure karesansui garden of gravel and boulders, such as that at Norwich cathedral. Even here the setting cannot reflect a setting in Japan.

Despite the various constraints on interpretation there is no doubt that the Japanese garden tradition is a deep wellspring of potential inspiration. The Western garden is eminently suited to adapting many of the ideas and design concepts used in Japan and study of the 'Aspects of Japanese gardens' referred to elsewhere (pages 19-31) can suggest the underlying characteristics to which attention must be paid. Many of these can be interpreted in a Western setting. The result can be a garden that has the 'feel' of a Japanese garden but is well adapted to our architecture and climate.

TOP: Detail of the karesansui garden constructed in 2010 at Norwich Cathedral (IC).

RIGHT: Private garden in Manchester showing Japanese use of space and a few boulders, but with mixed planting in European style to create a 'Japanese feel' (GH).

TOP and RIGHT: Private garden in Manchester designed and constructed by the owner, a member of the Japanese Garden Society (Heather Wright).

practical issues

There is little doubt that climate affects our gardens differently from those in Japan. Many plants grown in Japan are not hardy enough to grow well or at all here in Britain. Substitute planting material has to be used, which inevitably brings a different visual and textural quality.

Nursery businesses are significantly different in the two countries. In Japan it is perfectly normal to be able to buy 50 or 100 year old pruned trees and very large shaped shrubs. Gardens are constructed in their finished state using large trees and shrubs. Our nursery business does not have a history of growing and shaping such plant material and typically we plant young plants and trees, the finished garden only emerging after many years.

In Japan the garden and its associated building are inextricably linked, the building seems to be part of the garden and *vice versa*. This presents design issues in juxtaposing a garden from the Japanese culture with typical British architecture, making it harder to replicate the 'feel' of a Japanese garden.

Maintenance of Japanese gardens requires special skills, particularly in pruning. Garden cleaning and tidying on a daily basis is the norm for most domestic gardens in Japan. In the UK there is no doubt that the more successful Japanese gardens are those that benefit from the necessary maintenance regime.

TOP: Azaleas being clipped at Shisen-do in Kyoto. Careful and time consuming maintenance is essential for the best appearance of Japanese gardens. Note the size of the Azaleas, difficult to achieve in the UK climate (GH).

OPPOSITE: Moving a pine tree – Yushien garden, Matsue, Japan. All tree stock in Japan is sold and kept in rootballs so that, as here, the tree can be lifted and moved at any time. Our UK nurseries are not geared up to providing mature trees in this form (GH).

japanese-style gardens in the uk and ireland

open to the public

The gardens indicated on the map opposite represent a selection of Japanese gardens that are open to the public in the UK and Ireland. There are many more gardens that have the label 'Japanese Garden' that have not been included.

The selection shown includes the most significant or important Japanese landscape gardens. It omits gardens that have only a small area in them or a feature that makes them 'Japanese' and those that are simply collections of Japanese plants.

There are other gardens that are open to the public once a year such as Cottered garden in Hertfordshire, a privately owned but important historic garden.

Visitors should verify that gardens are open before they visit.

Many gardens have their own website where full details can be obtained.

selected japanese gardens in the uk and ireland

Scotland
Lauriston Castle, Edinburgh
St Mungo Zen Garden, Glasgow
Stobo Japanese Water Garden, Peeblesshire

Northern England
Calderstones Park, Liverpool
Horsforth Park, Leeds
Pure Land, Nottinghamshire
Tatton Park, Cheshire
Walkden Gardens, Sale, Cheshire

Midlands and East Anglia
Newstead Abbey, Nottinghamshire
Birmingham Botanical Gardens
Danescourt Cemetery, Wolverhampton
Momotaro garden, Spalding, Lincolnshire
Norwich Cathedral
Warwick University Arts Building Courtyard (by appointment)

Republic of Ireland
Tully Japanese Garden, Co. Kildare

Wales
National Botanic Garden of Wales, Carmarthenshire

London and South East
Capel Manor Gardens, Essex
Fanhams Hall, Hertfordshire
Gatton Park, Reigate, Surrey
Hammersmith Park, London
Kyoto Garden, Holland Park, London
Royal Botanic Gardens, Kew, London
University of London School of Oriental and African Studies (SOAS) Roof Garden

South West
The Bonsai Nursery, St Mawgan, Cornwall
Compton Acres, Poole, Dorset
Dartington Hall Gardens, Devon
Kingston Lacy, Dorset
Pine Lodge Gardens, St Austell, Cornwall

individual gardens

A selection of individual gardens is shown here in more detail. Appreciation of these gardens is to a large extent subjective and this particular selection is not intended to identify 'the best' gardens merely to reflect the wide range of gardens and their different styles that are open to the public It includes some of historic interest and value as well as very recently constructed gardens.

Pine Lodge Gardens, St Austell, Cornwall

Pine Lodge Gardens provides excellent growing conditions for rare, unusual and tender plants, the collection now standing at well over 6,000 plants, all labelled, in over 30 acres of gardens.
The Japanese garden, which uses Shakkei (borrowed scenery), was added in the early 2000s (Pine Lodge Gardens).

Compton Acres, Poole, Dorset

Compton Acres was built in 1924 and is a wonderful example of a historic garden in the UK. Spread over 10 acres it has seven distinct gardens, including an Italian Garden and a Japanese Garden.
The Japanese garden, set in an enclosed valley, is a classic design enriched by many azaleas, with a Tea House that is wisteria clad in May (GH).
Website: www.comptonacres.co.uk

National Botanic Garden of Wales

The Real Japanese Garden was brought to the 568 acre Garden of Wales from the Chelsea 2001 Flower Show where it won a gold medal and 'Best in Show'. It consists of three traditional Japanese gardens - a Stream and Lake Garden, a Gravel Garden and a Tea Garden.
The Garden was designed by Professor Masao Fukuhara, a lecturer in design at Osaka University, and the Professor and his team supervised the installation of the Japanese Garden at NBGW (National Botanic Garden of Wales).
Website: www.gardenofwales.org.uk

Birmingham Botanical Gardens

The Garden is a Courtyard Garden or 'tsubo-niwa' (garden between buildings), and was built with the help of members of the Japanese Garden Society. It contains elements of several garden styles. Adjacent to the Japanese Courtyard is a fine display of hardy bonsai trees opened in April 1993, and is a joint venture between the Botanical Gardens and the Friends of the National Bonsai Collection (GH).
Website: www.birminghambotanicalgardens.co.uk

Royal Botanic Gardens, Kew, London

In addition to its unparalleled collection of plants from all over the world, Kew Gardens has a Japanese landscape consisting of three garden areas designed to give an impression of some of the many different aspects of Japanese gardens.
They were opened in 1996 and are centred around a Japanese Gateway, Chokushi-Mon, a replica (four-fifths actual size) of the Karamon at Nishi Honganji in Kyoto, created for the Japan-British Exhibition in 1910 and presented to Kew in 1911 (GB).
Website: www.kew.org

·lammersmith Park, London

'he Park is what little remains of the site of the apan-British Exhibition of 1910. Part of the 'Garden)f Peace' from the exhibition still exists, but had)een reduced in size and somewhat modified.
'he 2010 renovation was aimed at giving the existing garden a more authentic Japanese feel and by adding Japanese inspired' elements elsewhere in the park it s no longer an isolated feature (GB).

The Kyoto Garden in Holland Park, London

Holland Park is about 22 hectares (54.36 acres) in area and is considered one of the most romantic and peaceful parks of central London.
In 1991 a team of Japanese gardeners was sponsored by Kyoto Chamber of Commerce to transform part of the woodland area into an attractive Japanese garden. Named 'The Kyoto Garden', it was opened in 1991 to celebrate the Japanese Festival, and refurbished in 2001 as part of Japan 2001 (GB).

Pure Land Meditation Centre and Japanese Garden, North Clifton, Nottinghamshire

The Pure Land Meditation Centre is run by Buddha Maitreya (Koji Takeuchi). After completing an MA in Buddhist Theology and spending some time as a Zen Buddhist monk he founded Pure Land in 1973 as a base from which to teach meditation. In 1980 Maitreya began transforming two acres of wilderness into a Japanese garden. His main aim was to provide a peaceful, beautiful area which guests and visitors to the centre could enjoy (IC).
Website: www.buddhamaitreya.co.uk

Sainsbury Institute Japanese Garden at Norwich Cathedral

A Japanese karesansui garden - The Garden of Calm Virtue (Tokuon no niwa) - has been built in the consecrated ground of Norwich Cathedral. The Sainsbury Institute Japanese Garden links the 11th century cathedral to the newly opened Hostry built on the original monastic ground, and offers all visitors a moment for contemplation as they enter the cathedral. The garden was designed by Graham Hardman and Robert Ketchell and constructed by members of the Japanese Garden Society (GH).
Website: www.sainsbury-institute.org

The Sainsbury Institute Japanese Garden - the Garden of Calm Virtue (Tokuon no niwa) at Norwich Cathedral (Kaz Morohashi)

Danescourt Cemetery, Wolverhampton

Designed by Peter Bridge in 1996, the garden provides a source of contemplation and meditation. The garden is divided asymmetrically by a central wall which creates two contrasting gardens. One is based on a 'Dry' Garden, the other on a traditional Tea Garden, with stepping stones, lanterns and a water basin.
The planting beyond the walls contains the eye within the site whilst giving the impression of depth (RIGHT and OPPOSITE: GH).

St Mungo Museum of Religious Life and Art, Glasgow

The Museum is located beside Glasgow Cathedral. Despite being named after St Mungo, Glasgow's patron saint, it tries to cover all religions - the first object that visitors see is an authentic dry stone Japanese Zen Garden, claimed to be the first of its kind in the UK.
It was designed for the Museum by Mr Yasutaro Tanaka, vice-president of Kyoto's Landscape Association in 1993 (GH).

The Bonsai Nursery, St Mawgan, Cornwall

After successfully establishing the Bonsai Nursery, Robert and Stella Hore turned their attention to the creation of the Japanese Garden in 1991, taking six years to develop the extensive garden that we see today.
The garden, set in a wooded valley, contains many separate areas - a moss garden, bamboo grove, several ponds, a waterfall, a tea house, various gateways and fences and a karesansui (dry garden) (The Bonsai Nursery).
Website: www.thebonsainursery.com

Walkden Gardens, Sale, Cheshire

Designed and constructed by members of the Japanese Garden Society between 2004 and 2006, this garden is part of Walkden Gardens, a public park administered by Trafford Borough Council.
The garden is an attempt to create the feel of a garden as it might be seen in Japan, using design ideas commonly used in the Japanese garden tradition (GH).
Website: www.walkdengardens.co.uk

The view from the waiting arbour in the Japanese garden at Walkden Gardens in Sale, Cheshire, public gardens managed by Trafford Borough Council (GH).

Walkden Gardens, with the waiting arbour on the left. The garden was formally opened by the Japanese Ambassador in October 2006 (GH).

Lauriston Castle, Edinburgh

The grounds of Lauriston Castle, standing in 30 acres enjoying a magnificent view across the Firth of Forth, are maintained by Edinburgh City Council, and are open to the public as a public park.
The Edinburgh – Kyoto Friendship Garden is a Japanese garden built to celebrate the twinning of Edinburgh and the Japanese prefecture of Kyoto. It was designed and built by Takashi Sawano and opened in August 2002 (Alison, Edinburgh Spotlight).

Tatton Park, Knutsford, Cheshire

The 50 acres of gardens at Tatton have been developing for over 200 years. The Japanese Garden was almost certainly the result of Alan de Tatton's visit to the Japan-British Exhibition at the White City in London in 1910.
A team of Japanese workmen joined the Tatton gardeners to create what is now considered by some to be the "finest example of a Japanese Garden in Europe."
The garden was restored in 2000/2001 for the Japan Festival by Professor Fukuhara of Osaka University (GH).
Website: www.tattonpark.org.uk

ABOVE: . Laursiton Castle , Edinburgh, showing the 'shakkei' or borrowed scenery of the Firth of Forth. The garden was designed by Takashi Sawano and opened in 2002 (Alison, Edinburgh Spotlight).

RIGHT: Gateway at Tatton Park following the restoration of the 1911 garden in 2001 (IC).

Private Garden, Kent. Constructed in the early 1920s and based on a design from Josiah Conder's Landscape Gardening in Japan (IC).